This book is presented to

With love from

Date

The BLESSING

of a FATHER'S LOVE

IDEALS PUBLICATIONS • NASHVILLE, TENNESSEE

ISBN 0-8249-5878-0

Published by Ideals Publications, a division of Guideposts
535 Metroplex Drive, Suite 250, Nashville, Tennessee 37211
www.idealsbooks.com

Printed and bound in Mexico by RR Donnelley

Compiled and edited by Peggy Schaefer
Designed by Marisa Calvin
Cover photograph by Monserrate J. Schwartz/Alamy

1 3 5 7 9 10 8 6 4 2

ACKNOWLEDGMENTS

ANTHENAT, KATHY SMITH, for "A Letter to My Father." BOWLER, ARTHUR, for "Indelible Love Marked the Pages."
FRANTZ, ELAINE C., for "And So Much More." FULGHUM, HUNTER S. "Dinosaurs" from *Like Father, Like Son* by Hunter
S. Fulghum, copyright © 1996 by the author, published by G. P. Putnam's Sons. REAGAN, MAUREEN. An excerpt from
First Father, First Daughter: A Memoir by Maureen Reagan, copyright © 1989 by MER Inc. Published by Little Brown
& Co. SECUNDA, VICTORIA. "A doting father . . ." from *Women and Their Fathers* by Victoria Secunda, published by
Delacorte Press, 1992. VIORST, JUDITH. An excerpt from *Necessary Losses* by Judith Viorst. Copyright © 1986. Used by
permission of Simon & Schuster. Every effort has been made to establish ownership and use of each selection in this
book. If contacted, the publisher will be pleased to rectify any inadvertent errors or omissions in subsequent editions.

Photography Credits: Page 9, Holt Studios International/Alamy; pages 10–11, VStock/Alamy; page 24, Dennis Frates;
page 28, Stock Connection Distribution/Alamy; pages 32–33, Dennis Frates; page 37, Jiang Jin/SuperStock; page 38,
ImageState/Alamy; page 45, George and Monserrate Schwartz/Alamy; pages 50–51, age fotostock/SuperStock; page 53,
Arcaid/Alamy; page 55, Alaska Stock LLC/Alamy; pages 56–57, Joe Sohm/Alamy; page 60, IMAGINA The Image
Maker/Alamy.

A FATHER'S LOVE
IS STRONG IN ITS GENTLENESS,
GENTLE IN ITS STRENGTH.
IT HELPS A CHILD
TO REACH NEW HEIGHTS
OF HAPPINESS,
NEW DEPTHS OF UNDERSTANDING,
NEW DIMENSIONS OF LIFE.
—AUTHOR UNKNOWN

A Father's
Love . . .

inspires

Small boys become big men through the influence
of big men who care about small boys.

—AUTHOR UNKNOWN

I learned from the example of my father
that the manner in which one endures
what must be endured is more important
than the thing that must be endured.

—DEAN ACHESON

THE VIEW FROM DAD'S KNEE

Melinda Rathjen

I still remember the view from Dad's riding lawn mower. When Dad put his "cut-grass shoes" on, my brother, sister, and I would follow him out to the front lawn and help him clear the yard of small limbs and the four rubber baseball bases. Then we'd stand on the front porch, waving our thumbs up and down, up and down, in our own special version of a hitchhiker's signal, while he mowed, dodging blue spruce and pine trees, spiraling inward in his precise pattern. Sometimes we wandered off to play in the backyard or inside, coming back to watch as he cut the

grass even shorter in the base paths.

When Dad finished cutting, unable to resist his three little hitchhikers, he would turn off the mower's blade, drive over to us, and take each of us, in our turn, for a ride in a wide loop around the front yard. The view was unbeatable.

Dad has always lived the way he cut the grass. A diligent worker, he is also diligent about taking the time to enjoy and love his family. I will always be thankful for the outlook on life that I found in the view from Dad's knee.

I watched a small man with thick calluses on both hands work fifteen and sixteen hours a day. I saw him once literally bleed from the bottoms of his feet, a man who came here uneducated, alone, unable to speak the language, who taught me all I needed to know about faith and hard work by the simple eloquence of his example.

—MARIO CUOMO

Our father presents an optional set of rhythms and responses for us to connect to. As a second home base, he makes it safer to roam. With him as an ally— a love—it is safer, too, to show that we're mad when we're mad at our mother. We can hate and not be abandoned, hate and still love.

—JUDITH VIORST

I never could be
thankful enough that
my father was honest and simple,
and that his love of truth and justice
had grown into his being
as naturally as the oaks
were rooted to the earth
along the little stream.

—CLARENCE DARROW

INDELIBLE LOVE MARKED THE PAGES

Arthur Bowler

I watched intently as my little brother was caught in the act. He sat in the corner of the living room, a pen in one hand and my father's brand-new hymn book in the other.

As my father walked into the room, my brother cowered slightly; he sensed that he had done something wrong. From a distance I could see that he had opened my father's new hymnal and scribbled in it the length and breadth of the first page with a pen.

Now, staring at my father fearfully, he and I both waited for his punishment.

My father picked up his prized hymnal, looked at it carefully, and then sat down, without saying a word. Books were precious to him; he was a clergyman and the holder of several degrees.

What he did next was remarkable. Instead of punishing my brother, instead of scolding or yelling or reprimanding, he sat down, took the pen from my brother's hand, and then wrote in the book himself, alongside the scribbles John had made:

John's work, 1959, age 2

From time to time we would open it, look at the scribbles, read my father's expression of love, and feel uplifted. Now I know that through this simple act my father taught us how every event in life has a positive side—if we are prepared to look at it from another angle—and how precious it is when our lives are touched by little hands.

A FATHER'S
LOVE . . .

comforts

There is no one like a father to care so completely,
give so quietly, teach so gently, love so much.

—Author Unknown

A father's love is evident in countless ways,
many of them nonverbal.

—P.S. Biel

FIRST FATHER, FIRST DAUGHTER

Maureen Reagan

I have very specific memories of my father tiptoeing into my room when I was supposed to be asleep. He'd peek over at me to see if I was awake (which I always was), in a way that was almost conspiratorial, and then he'd sit himself down and read me a story. My favorites were the fairy tales of Hans Christian Andersen, though once in a while I'd get a dose of the Brothers Grimm, which I found a little too spooky for my young tastes. Sometimes, too, I'd be treated to my father's stories about his own growing up, which to me were as wonderful as anything penned by any writer. He'd sit with his legs crossed in a chair over by the window, and whether the stories were his or someone else's, I would listen anxiously from my pillow, not wanting to miss a word.

But whatever the story, he'd always cap it off with my favorite bedtime song. . . .

We had a little game worked out about that song. "Please, Daddy," I would threaten playfully, "I won't go to sleep until you sing to me."

And then he'd start in, with a soft, deep, and soothing baritone that could lull any daughter to dreamland in ten hot seconds.

Father—a son's first hero, a daughter's first love.

—Proverb

*Every parent is at some time the father of
the unreturned prodigal, with nothing to do
but keep his house open to hope.*

—John Ciardi

FATHERLY DUTIES

Todd Wilson

It was one of those nights when I love being a dad. There I was, staring into the black night, blinded by the head-lights of the oncoming traffic. I refused to blink, tightened my grip on the steering wheel, and resolved to get us through. The only noise I heard was the hypnotic sound of car tires on the pavement and an occasional grunt from my wife. In the rearview mirror were the still figures of our chil-dren surrounded by the toys and books that we had brought along. . . .

Driving the family is my job, as it was my dad's before

me. Not long ago I was the one who slept while he manned the wheel. The road noise was just as hypnotic then as it is now. On one occasion, I can remember a long day of driving to some place like North Carolina or Florida. . . . As the sun set, a stillness invaded the car until, one by one, my mom, siblings, and I fell asleep. Yet Dad drove on through the night.

I can remember more than once being awakened from sleep by some passing truck or pothole in the road. . . . In the driver's seat, staring at black road, was my dad, quietly doing what we all expected him to do. I'd sit in silence and watch my dad as a sailor might watch the captain at the helm during a storm. He never seemed to tire; yet looking back, I know he must have been exhausted. He never complained or asked my mother to relieve him of his post. After all, he was the dad.

protects

I cannot think of any need in childhood as strong as the need for a father's protection.

—SIGMUND FREUD

When I was a kid, I used to imagine animals running under my bed. I told my dad, and he solved the problem quickly. He cut the legs off the bed.

—LOU BROCK

AND SO MUCH MORE

Elaine C. Frantz

A baby girl is born. Instantaneously, from amid the ranks of ordinary men, there emerges a courageous, fearless, and gallant man who is quaking in his shoes. He holds the newborn to his heart. In the years to come, the child will call him Father. As time goes by, she will come to know that this man is the most extraordinary individual with whom she will ever have the pleasure of being acquainted. . . .

He is no ordinary man who always lives in a state of becoming; who is continually learning from his children;

who is made richer by the sight of his children coming home; who teaches that all the pros and cons must be weighed before a decision is made; who stands willingly ready to experience all that he has never done before; who is able to inspire monumental achievements in her; who faces no problems in his life, only difficult situations which are the portals of discovery; who is constantly called upon to be the very strongest one; and who provides the ever-present base to touch when her world is full of confusion and question.

One night a father overheard
his son pray: "Dear God,
make me the kind of man my daddy is."
Later that night, the father prayed,
"Dear God, make me the kind of man
my son wants me to be."

—AUTHOR UNKNOWN

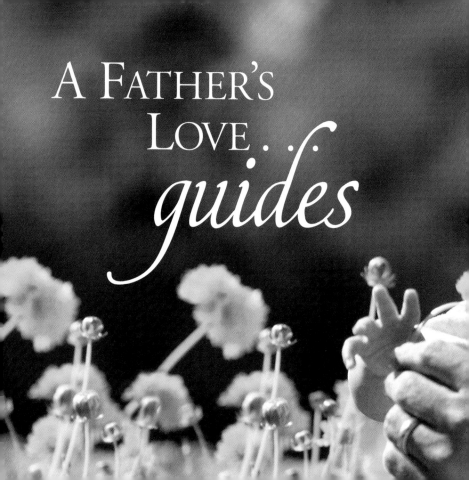

A Father's
Love...
guides

My father was my hero,
and I watched his every move with admiration
and a desire to emulate what he did.

—Jimmy Carter

A father is a man who expects his children to be
as good as he meant to be.

—Carol Coats

A LETTER TO MY FATHER

Kathy Smith Anthenat

I just want to say "thank you."

Thank you for teaching us how to hold an important decision in our fist like a ball of dirt and test it to see if it is ready for our plow. Thank you for adversity that kept us from growing up too spindly like a tomato seedling that has had too much water and not enough hot sun. Thank you for shouldering duties in life, like burying the family dog, until we were old enough to do them. Thank you for caring more about the cleanliness of our morals than of our faces. Thank you for the type of childhood which seems to be get-

ting squeezed out in the technological shuffle. Thank you for my appreciation of quiet moments, spring rains, and cedar Christmas trees.

Today I celebrate my good fortune in having you for a father.

He didn't tell me how to live;
he lived, and let me watch him do it.

—CLARENCE BUDINGTON KELLAND

A father sees his children as God sees all of us;
he looks into the very depths of their hearts;
he knows their intentions. . . .

—HONORÉ DE BALZAC

THE VALUE OF WHY

Enid Black

When my dad was a student, he excelled in all subjects but especially loved mathematics. He often purchased math textbooks just to see if he could work the exercises.

I did not inherit my father's penchant for numbers. Instead, I struggled with math and bombarded him each night with questions about my homework.

My father answered each question with patience. He didn't try to make me love the subject the way that he did; instead, he told me that math was an exercise for my brain. Even if I never solved the problems, working them would help me learn to think in different ways. The exercise would strengthen my mind and help me in the other subjects that I enjoyed the most. If I told him that I couldn't work a problem, he would listen to my approaches and make suggestions, but he would not accept the word "can't."

I don't remember too many math facts these days, but I will never forget the lessons I learned from my father. As he mentored me on those frustrating evenings, he taught me to embrace the challenge that a problem provides and to persevere, no matter what the obstacle.

A FATHER'S
LOVE . . .

endures

DAD'S LOVE IN PICTURES

Christopher Riley

One hallway in my parents' house tells the true story of how my dad shows his love. The wall is covered with pictures of my sister and me, beginning on the left with images of us in the baby bathtub and ending, for now, with photos our parents took as we moved into our dorm rooms.

I love these pictures because they're not formal portraits but snapshots of everyday moments. They remind me that my dad is always with me when it matters the most, not just for special occasions but also when no one expects him to be there. In one picture, my dad feeds me puréed bananas as my

mom fixes pancakes in the background. In another, Dad and I smile goofily under the paper sailor hats that we made together. Framed in Popsicle sticks is an image of my dad helping my sister and me wrap presents for my grandmother's birthday.

Someday, God willing, pictures of my own sons and daughters will decorate a hallway in my house. I hope that my children will gaze at the cluster of images and feel the same rush of love for their father that I do for mine.

Fathers have very stout hearts,
so they have to be broken sometimes or
no one would know what's inside of them.

—AUTHOR UNKNOWN

Real fathering is not biological—it is the conscious
choice to build an unconditional and unbreakable
connection to another human being.

—WILL GLENNON

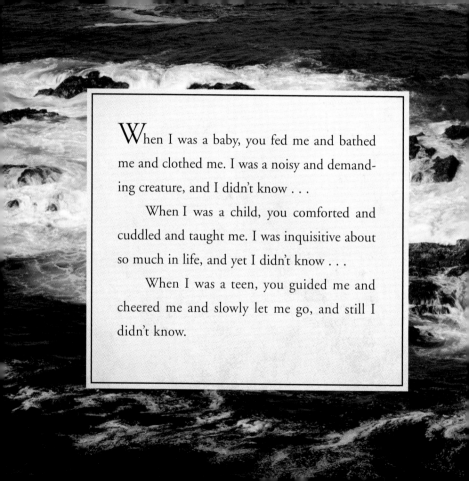

When I was a baby, you fed me and bathed me and clothed me. I was a noisy and demanding creature, and I didn't know . . .

When I was a child, you comforted and cuddled and taught me. I was inquisitive about so much in life, and yet I didn't know . . .

When I was a teen, you guided me and cheered me and slowly let me go, and still I didn't know.

I didn't know about the sleepless nights and countless diaper changes.

I didn't know how you sometimes had to re-teach yourself in order to teach me.

I didn't know how you longed to hold me just a bit longer, while I longed to run free.

I didn't know at what cost you gave me every ounce of love you possessed.

Only now am I beginning to know . . .

—P.S. Biel

Dinosaurs

Hunter S. Fulghum

There is a spot in southeastern Utah where the rocks have been weathered by millions of years of wind and rain and cold and heat. Scattered along the edge, where the green rock and the layers above it meet, you can see dinosaur tracks.

I spent a morning tracing these steps, completely caught up in the excitement of each moment. My father and I called to each other as we found new sets of prints. And as the afternoon approached, we sat down on a rock that bore the rippled imprint of an ancient shore.

We spoke of the past and the future. My father talked about my grandfather, a man I never knew. He told me stories about growing up in Texas, riding horses, being my age in a different time and place.

Somewhere in the stories, there was a sense of his handing me the past, not just of his life, but of all things and creatures that had come before—the dinosaurs, the Indians, the father, and the grandfather. All of them converge, for now in some measure, in me, in the twisting path that is our history and heritage. My own children have taken the leading edge of this wave of life. Someday perhaps I will tell them stories about their grandfather and times long ago, and one afternoon spent sitting on a rock, chasing dinosaur tracks, and marveling at the wonder of it all.

It's only when you grow up, and step back from him, or leave him for your own career and your own home—it's only then that you can measure his greatness and fully appreciate it. Pride reinforces love.

—MARGARET TRUMAN